1

Shark
On Line

By

Carla Allen

ISBN: 1470090848
ISBN-13: 978-1470090845

Acknowledgements

Special thanks to many – to Fred Hatfield, who asked me if I'd ever considered being a reporter, then hired me to cover stories that changed and shaped my life; to Tina Comeau, Eric Bourque and Mike Gorman, the best friend-mentors in the world; to Brent Kempton, for constant encouragement. As well, Steven Campana and Art Gaetan for their fascinating interviews on shark research and fishing.

Contents

Audrey McDonald wins the first
Yarmouth Shark Scramble in 1998.

Chapter 1 – Baiting the hooks

The sight is not for the squeamish. Long and lean and dripping with blood, each shark is wrestled from a vessel's hold and hoisted high to dangle from a scale.

Research scientists and students move in to slice open the belly and examine the contents after the catch is lowered to the dock. They cut and peer, measure and record.

At several Nova Scotia (NS) ports these scenes have become an annual occurrence. They generate excitement and provide greater insight into a creature that has fascinated and instilled fear in mankind for centuries.

The shark fishing tournaments and derbies at Jeddore, Arichat, Riverport, Halifax, Brooklyn, Lockeport and Yarmouth are typically held in late summer when water temperatures are higher.

Participants must purchase a Department of Fisheries and Oceans recreational shark fishing license and only sharks over eight feet can be kept. Although blue sharks, known locally as blue dogs, are the most populous species, mako, thrashers and porbeagles are sometimes landed.

Fishermen are required to record the length, weight, sex and location of every shark that is caught, even those that are released because of inadequate size. They're also requested to tag the fish before returning it to the sea. The tagging is proving to be a valuable aid to scientists.

In addition to assisting research, the Yarmouth Shark Scramble helps out the community. Since its start in 1998, the event has served as a fundraiser for several organizations, pouring at least $70,000 into coffers.

Juniper House (a women's shelter), Skate Yarmouth, the HOPE Centre, Crime Stoppers, Yarmouth County Ground Search & Rescue, Yarmouth Development Corporation, and PLAY Yarmouth are a few of the non-profit organizations that have benefitted from the Shark Scramble.

Shark Scramble founder Bob Gavel.

The roots of the Yarmouth event trace back to Bob Gavel. He'd heard about a shark fishing tournament in Eastern Passage, N.S. and travelled there to check it out. After seeing large crowds and the number of participants he decided to try to start a similar event for this region.

" I thought something like that would be good for Yarmouth seeing as we hadn't had much since the tuna fishing tournament had stopped," he said.

From 1935 to the mid 1960's, Wedgeport, NS, was the sport tuna fishing capital of the world. An abundance of small fish attracted the Bluefin tuna close to the shores of Wedgeport, with the Tusket River and the Tuna Rip recognized as excellent tuna fishing grounds.

In 1949, 72 Bluefin tuna were caught during the International Tuna Cup Match making a total weight of 30,161 lbs. The tournament ended in South West Nova in 1976 due to smaller catches.

Gavel started looking around for people to help him get the event off the ground. Some of the original committee members were Steve and Doreen Brannon, Brian and Donna Smith, Bobby Newell, Russell Deveau, Irving Deveau, John Boudreau, Norman LeBlanc and Ray and Louise Zinck.

Gavel knew that some of these people had attended shark fishing tournaments in other areas and that several had fished shark recreationally. Each year, the committee began organizing the event in February in order to get everything in place for August.

By 2003 the tournament had grown into a giant, with 50 boats registered and 348 participants. Eighty-five sharks were caught, including two makos. Gavel estimates 10,000 people visited the weekend event at that time.

A giant tuna is hoisted from the hold.

In 2004, members from the Wedgeport community, impressed by the growth and draw of the Yarmouth Shark Scramble, approached its committee to brainstorm. That year, the tuna tournament was reinstated to coincide with the shark scramble.

Display boards promoting Wedgeport's historic fishing era and the re-birth of the fishing competition were erected on the Yarmouth waterfront during the shark tournament. A shuttle bus ran between the two events.

It had been 28 years since the tuna tournament had last been held. Sad-ly, no fish were caught that year. But Wedgeport did not give up. The following year, two bluefin were landed. In 2008, 16 bluefin tuna were landed. In 2011, the catch totaled 3,338 pounds.

"We took pride in helping them to get that going again. It's good not only for the Yarmouth community, it's good for Wedgeport. All com-munities need to work together to make things happen," said Gavel, who stepped down from the shark scramble committee after his 10th year but continued as a fishing participant.

As time went on, changes were made and gradually there was a decline in popularity with fewer registrations. In 2007, the 10th anniversary, it was decided to spread the event over four days, starting Wednesday with optional departure times and two-day time periods in which to catch sharks. Participants had the option of departing right after the captains' meeting at 7 p.m. on Wednesday.

There are several opinions on the effect of the lengthened event. John Boudreau, who has organized the event since then, believes it to be an improvement as it provides fishermen a window of opportunity for weather and safety.

"You have the option of leaving on either day and you have a 48-hour window to go and get back. A lot of fishermen who used to go out on smaller vessels have opted to join others on bigger boats.

Sharks cover the dock during the annual Yarmouth Shark Scramble.

It's more comfortable and the other guys need help to pay for the fuel and such. They all chip in. You have to go so far and in a small boat you can only go out a short ways," he said.

Gavel says he's heard from people that the time span and distance has dissuaded participants, especially those who have a tendency towards seasickness. The distance requires more crewmen amongst the fishermen onboard who can help stand watch.

Some people had to take vacation days for the mid-week start and it also cost more for fuel and other resources.

" We always travelled to Georges Banks, which is 10-12 hours steam, one way. You're up all night going out. If you wanted to compete and catch the larger shark, that's where you had to go, because that's where the largest sharks are," said Gavel.

"I think once they started switching to the middle of the week and going out overnight, it started to become a bit too much. They still have a turnout, but it's nowhere near what it used to be. I think with some small, minor changes it could come back as big as it ever was," he said.

At that time also, new conservation measures came into effect with boats limited to three sharks each, with a minimum length of eight feet. Nineteen boats participated that year.

In 2007, during the traditional captains' meeting held before the boats depart, the participants were presented with some of the information that the Bedford Institute of Oceanography (BIO) had collected over the years. Boudreau told the competitors that 125 small sharks were tagged and released in 2006.

"Last year they (BIO) had a map at the captains' meeting and they showed us how far some of the sharks went. They tracked one 1,500 miles from Yarmouth heading east. It was quite interesting," Boudreau said.

13

Warren Joyce removes a redfish from a shark's stomach.

Warren Joyce, a shark technician for the Marine Fish Division of DFO, has supervised the research conducted during the event in years past. The derbies provide an opportunity for teaching biology students, and gathering data about shark species. He and his students usually attend between four and six events annually in the province.

"Yarmouth compares with Lockeport with regard to size and number of sharks landed. In terms of overall operation I believe Yarmouth has the greatest turnout of people.

"Sharks really attract the public, whether it's out of interest or out of fear, I'm not really sure, but sharks really fascinate people," he said.

The generous prizes supplied by sponsors of the Yarmouth event no doubt play a part in attracting fishermen. For every 20 pounds of shark caught, competitors receive an extra ballot for the grand prize, which is awarded in a random draw. During the elimination event 20 names are drawn for prizes, starting at $100 and climbing to $1500 with $10,000 in total. The last prize drawn is the grand prize and in past years the recipient has received a trip for two to a southern destination.

Some of the funds contributed to the local charities come from the sale of the shark meat. Shark sales were experimental in the beginning, says Boudreau.

"We tried to sell the meat of the blue dog shark. For the first few years you'd make 15 or 20 cents a pound for human consumption, around $700-$1,500 total, but the meat ammoniates. They pee through their skin. After they're caught it's not long after that they give off the ammonia smell. Now, if you can get rid of it (sharks), you sell it for mink or dog food. We pretty well have to give it away," he said.

The lean meat is best marinated and grilled. However, in Iceland, a traditional recipe for shark (Hakari) entails letting the meat rot for six months to expel toxic chemicals. As the meat decomposes, it oozes toxic ammonia.

Most people would likely prefer the preparation methods of Chef Martin Picard and sous-chef Hugue Dufour from the Food Network's television show *Wild Chef.*

15

During the Seafest fish feast in Yarmouth,
shark steak was a popular item for sampling.

They filmed an episode during the 2010 tournament in Yarmouth.

Before trying to land the "predator of his dream" Picard collected dulse, knotted wrack, Irish moss, and seashore plantain with Dufour from the region's French Shore for a seaweed salad that included red onion, salt and vinegar, and chives cured in brine.
The celebrity chefs sailed aboard *Whispering Sea V* with Captain Tim Nickerson. Biologist Warren Joyce asked the men to record measurements of the shark before they prepared it for cooking.

Picard inserted lard into the shark steak before searing it in oil. He topped it with a blend of parsley, bread crumbs and garlic and baked it for one hour. With the remaining oil he whipped in mustard, the zest of one lemon and a slosh of white wine.

The verdict? "I don't know if it's because the shark is very fresh, because he is young or very small, but never, never, have I tasted shark good like this one," he said.

Back on the wharf the chefs made shark temakis which included seasoned sushi rice, battered shark sticks, sabayon - made with white wine, egg yolks, minced pickles, shallots and capers with a side of matchstick potatoes. This was wrapped up in a sheet of nori, browned with a blowtorch and topped with a quail egg and salmon roe.

"If this is part of life, I'm ready for another 50 years," said Picard as the pair chowed down happily on the fare while sitting on a truck's tailgate.

Dufour said his son asked him for a shark necklace before he left home to participate in the event. He was presented with the necklace to give to his son before he left Yarmouth.

In 2011, 122 participants registered for the Yarmouth Shark Scramble. A *Land and Sea* crew filmed an episode during the event and *Canada in the Rough* shot footage. Participants have travelled from as far away as Iqaluit, Great Britain, U.S., Ontario and B.C.

For the shark temakis recipe, visit the *Food Network* (www.foodnetwork.ca/recipes/Rice/Grain/recipe.html?dishid=10734)

The U.S. Food and Drug Administration (www.fda.gov) recommends that pregnant women, women who might become pregnant, nursing mothers and young children avoid shark meat because of its potentially high mercury level. Others should moderate their consumption.

Jamie Doucette with the jaw of the 1,082-pound mako.

Chapter 2 - Shark capture is quite the fish story

By Shelley Fralic

When it hit, Jamie Doucette knew it was big. He was used to big, mind you, being a man who'd spent two decades on the Nova Scotia coast as a lobster fisherman, and being a regular entrant in the annual Yarmouth Shark Scramble, in which he once landed a nine-footer.

But this one, this one was different.

It's the first week in June and Doucette is standing on the dock in Wedgeport, a charming fishing village just south of Yarmouth, where his dad's lobster boat, *Soldier Boy II*, is back in the water after a good scrubbing, ready to head out for a summer of longline fishing for haddock, halibut and dogfish.

Doucette and his father fish for lobster from Shelburne to Digby, their traps scattered on the ocean floor as far out as the 50-mile limit, and it's out there you'll find them, father and son, every year from the last Monday in November until the end of May.

Doucette is 33, the poster boy for a new generation of Nova Scotia fishermen, from the pierced ears and tongue to the female pirate tattooed on his inner arm, from the tanned bald head and the neatly trimmed moustache and beard to the designer shades and the impressive biceps.

Under a hot sun, dressed in T-shirt, jeans and gumboots, he is recalling the day he caught the big fish, a short-fin mako shark so enormous it is still one of the largest ever caught on the planet.

It was August 2004 and he and a group of friends had taken a break from work and were in the annual scramble, enjoying a few beer on the back of his father-in-law's lobster boat.

The crew of the Pembroke Princess with their giant mako.

You might be surprised to hear there are mako sharks in Nova Scotia, but Doucette will tell you they are a regular visitor to Maritime waters, chasing mackerel with the Gulf Stream into the Bay of Fundy.

So there he was, fishing in the derby with a rod and reel, using a 200-pound test line and a hook baited with mackerel, chumming 48 miles out of Yarmouth.

"We were sitting in lawn chairs and having a couple of beer. We had a couple of hours to spare before we had to head back to the wharf.

"We had party balloons set out as bobbers on six rods, and as soon as we heard one of the lines zinging out, we reeled in the other lines and waited."

It was Doucette's line, and he worked it for 30 minutes before he saw the fin, rising a good foot out of the water about 150 yards out. His first thought? Great white. His second? Big.

Doucette was in a harness hooked to the rod, but there was no captain's chair bolting him down.

"If it decided to take off to Hong Kong, you're going with it."

After 15 more minutes of fight, the shark headed straight for the boat and, like a scene right out of Jaws, went under it.

"We're running around the boat so the line doesn't chafe, everyone's going crazy, running out of the way, and I had to keep handing off the rod. It went under the boat twice."

It was only then, an hour after he hooked it, that Doucette saw the mako. "It came up under the bow and rolled, belly up, and all I saw was white and I thought 'this sucker's big.' "

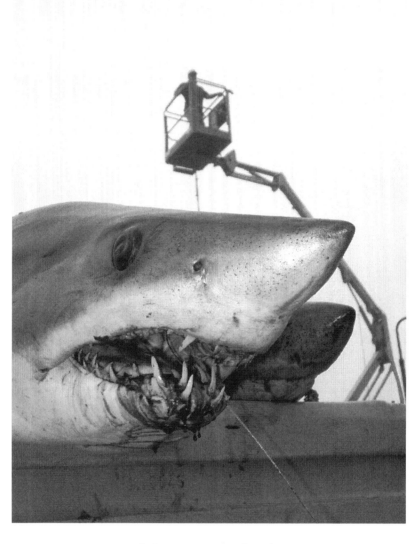

A fearsome set of teeth.

He handed off the rod and put on leather gloves just as the shark came around the stern, which on a lobster boat is open and about three feet off the water.

Doucette's friends started to get the ropes ready, intending to lasso the shark's tail, but couldn't because the fish was so big that the tail was out of reach.

Finally, one of them got a noose around its head but it chewed through it, thrashing and snapping its giant jaws at Doucette's feet. It bit through several more ropes until the crew finally secured it with three thicker ropes, wrapped around its huge head and lashed to a cleat. One of the crew eventually killed the shark by cutting its throat with an eight-inch knife; it bled out within minutes.

Doucette admits feeling a pang of guilt, hoping it wasn't a pregnant female, but knowing, too, that he had landed a great trophy.

It was so big that when they tried to haul it onto the boat using the boom and a portable hydraulic winch, the boom began to bend, forcing the men to abandon the winch and pull it on to the deck manually, using ropes.

With the shark finally secured, they headed back to shore, and Doucette phoned his mom and some friends and said: "You gotta come see this shark. It's huge."

"I thought it was maybe 400, 500 pounds, maybe 600. We couldn't get our arms around it."

They pulled up to the registry wharf in Yarmouth and as "soon as we hauled up the tarp and the boys saw the fin, everybody's jaw just dropped."

Jamie Doucette hoists his trophy high.

When they finally got it on the official scale, lifted into place by a fork-lift to keep the scale from tipping, the shark weighed in, to the growing crowd's delight, at an astonishing 1,082 pounds.

So big was this shark -- a Canadian record and one of the largest ever caught, its liver alone weighed 208 pounds -- that Doucette not only became a local celebrity, but the shark itself became an urban legend, with the Internet reporting that it was a great white and had been caught everywhere from Galveston, Tex. to Vancouver Island's Barkley Sound.

Doucette's fish was a female, measuring 10 feet, 11 inches and about 25 years old, according to scientists attending the derby, who said it had likely been mating and was probably fatigued at the time it was hooked. The mako's meat was sold to raise funds for local children's charities, and Doucette had a taxidermist friend mount the massive jaw. He took home about $3,500 in cash and prizes, along with the bragging rights that he carries today, which include a photo in Maxim magazine.

He missed the Shark Scramble last year, busy working and raising his young son, but says he will return because he is, by nature and nurture, a fisherman and because he has a title to defend.

"I love it. It's in me."

Material reprinted with the express permission of: The Vancouver Sun, a division of Postmedia Network Inc.

The fishing vessel *Shoal Hunter.*

Chapter 3 - Aboard the Shoal Hunter

Reprinted with permission from The Yarmouth Vanguard

"Let 'er happen, cap'n!" shouts a crewman. The sound of roaring engines powers up our excitement as vessels leave the dock together at five a.m. Sunday morning.

This group of 20 strong is the fast boat fleet, capable of doing 15 knots or more. We surge away from the wharf with a common goal – to catch the biggest shark of all.

There's the Cape Forchu lighthouse, its beacon the only part visible. Passing this landmark, we leave the sheltered waters of Yarmouth harbour to meet the open sea, still choppy from yesterday. A stiff crosswind adds considerable smack to our trip.

The throttles of all boats are shoved down hard as one and we spread out to race for warmer waters, preferred territory for sharks. Fishermen find these areas by consulting satellite photos on websites or by using boat thermometers.

Shoal Hunter's owner, Dana Robinson, shows me where I can brace myself on top of a gear locker in the wheelhouse. Spray obscures the view out side windows and my butt lifts off the locker as we smash through every wave. It will take three and a half hours for us to reach West of Teardrop, 50 miles at sea.

This is the sixth year for the Yarmouth Shark Scramble and the event continues to attract more interest. According to the DFO shark website, 16 sharks were landed in Yarmouth in 1998. The following year 106 were caught; in 2000 – 77; 2001 – 76 and last year 103.

Preparing the bait.

Robinson owns a fish plant in Parkers Cove, NS, as well as several other boats. Last year he never caught a shark but that hasn't stopped him from registering his boat and crew (cousin Capt. Jason Robinson, Alan Morrison and Jason Ellis) for this year.

As we near our destination, Morrison and Ellis begin rigging for shark. Stainless steel cable leaders, 80-pound test line and large hooks baited with a single mackerel are fastened to rods rented from Vernon D'Eon's for the weekend. Balloons are blown up and tied on, roughly 10 feet above the hooks, as bobbers. Bait is brought up from the hold, chopped and thrown in wire net chum baskets. Pails of beef and pork blood are set out to thaw.

We're over 100 fathoms when we cut the engine at 8:30 a.m.
The rods are stuck into side bits and tied tightly with rope. The ratcheting of the reels as line is paid out breaks the silence. The men trail the chum baskets off the stern and dangle pierced buckets of blood in the ocean. The water is cloudy with chum. It's impossible to look at the carnage and not think shark.

"Now comes the hard part," said Robinson. "Man, I hate waiting."
Hags and sea swallows feast on floating tidbits. The balloons bob lightly, instead of being yanked below the surface as we're hoping. We drift with the west-northwest wind pushing us sideways. The men settle back in their chairs and kill time.

They talk of barbecue sauce and drinking tequila and working on their woodlots. Ellis shouts for Morrison to put the Eagles CD on.

"Maybe that will work. You know, like Field of Dreams? Play it and they will come?" suggested Ellis.

Hotel California drifts out over the ocean. Sea swallows hop, skip and run on the surface as if they were dancing to the music. The balloons bob. I climb up on top of the wheelhouse and lay down on my back.

The men tie the rods in place.

It's warmer up here and the rocking of the boat almost puts me to sleep.

"Don't fall overboard," hollers one of the men. "A shark might get ya. The water's thick with 'em." Laughter. The men plunge the blood buckets up and down to release more fluid. Chum baskets are refilled. Seabirds flurry about, gobbling up more morsels. "We're going to get one today, guaranteed," declares Robinson. "Don't know if it's going to be this morning or this afternoon, even if I have to jump overboard to get it." The other men roar.

The radio chatter is depressing. "Boys, we just hooked a big one here. Just beginning to fight it... Got a 10 foot mako - nice and round... Hey we caught one with a hook already in it."

We can fish no later than 1:30 in order to make it back to Yarmouth by the deadline of 5 p.m.

The sharks have apparently decided to allow themselves to be hauled into other boats. We've poured about 70 gallons of blood into the sea, and donated approximately 100 pounds of cut-up squid and mackerel to the ocean ecology.

Just before leaving, a fin is spotted coming up fast behind us. SHARK!! The men run to the side of the boat and watch the fish swim to the stern and glide past to starboard. It isn't interested in our goodies.

Discouragement is a tangible emotion as the men busy themselves with storing rods, washing buckets and scrubbing the deck. We're not alone in our misery. Half of the 50 boats registered in the 2003 Yarmouth Shark Scramble did not catch a shark.

On Saturday, other participants caught 45 sharks for a total weight of 3,964 pounds. On Sunday, 38 sharks were landed with a total weight of 4,311. Chris Murphy aboard *Seahunter 1* caught the largest shark in the tournament.

Captain Dana Robinson

He fought with the 480-pound female mako for about an hour and a half before they hauled it aboard.

"It breached out of the water about three times. Came really close to the boat maybe six times and took off again, we had to bring it back. It was a good fight. We didn't take turns - they elected me to take the rod, I guess," he said.

"Some people helped in holding me up, helped me from falling over, helped make sure the line didn't get on the boat. We were all busy for the hour and a half. It was fun. It was quite a rush."
"We've been going for five years or so now. Some years we didn't catch any, some years we caught some."

As the *Shoal Hunter* is being tied to the wharf, Robinson says he'll probably go again next year.

"I really did it for these guys," he said, pointing to the crew. "If you see one caught, you'll see why we do it."

* * * *

Costs & Rewards

Cost to participate in the 2005 Shark Scramble:
Registration:$50 fee required from captain for boat
$100 for each person on board
Shark fishing license: $11.50 (each person must have one)
Fuel: Approximately $125.00
Food and drink: $75-several hundred
Bait: $12 per pail for blood
Mackerel 35 cents pound
Squid 70 cents pound
Weekend of lost revenue for fishermen

Rewards: $28,650 in cash and prizes.

Art Gaetan's shark fishing boat. Art Gaetan Photo

The rate of tooth replacement in some shark species
varies from once every eight to ten days to several months.
Photo courtesy Art Gaetan

Chapter 4 - Sharking with Art

When it comes to being hands on with sharks, Art Gaetan has laid his on thousands. Scientists may know a lot more about them on the technical side of things, he says, but he's your man for getting down and dirty with them.

Gaetan runs Blue Shark Fishing Charters, a sport fishing business out of Eastern Passage in Nova Scotia.

"I've been studying sharks, basically since I was old enough to read. I won't take anyone out if I don't believe they're going to get a fish. I go to catch fish," he says.

In 2011 they caught and released 589 sharks; in 2010 - 668. Gaetan draws on years of experience to teach his clients about fishing and ocean ecology on every trip. He's passionate about educating others about marine life and has taught legions of youngsters in schools through another enterprise he co-owned, called Oceans Wild.

He retired from the navy after 20 years and has fished fresh and salt-water species all over the world. He believes Atlantic Canada offers some of the most exciting salt-water fishing anywhere.

On a typical day he's up at 4 a.m. studying weather forecasts before he turns the keys on the boat. He checks Halifax approaches as well as the weather to the east and west because it might have an effect on the fishing later in the day, or if they hook into a large fish that's pulling them into that area of water.

Other factors are taken into consideration as well: the tides, how many he has on board, and where he's been in the past week. He doesn't like going any place two days in a row.

Excitement registers as the shark's reeled in.
Photo courtesy Art Gaetan

Hard to say what's on the line. Photo courtesy Art Gaetan

At 6 a.m. they cast off from the wharf aboard his boat, *Dig It*, a 34-foot Bayliner Sport Fisherman.

It takes about an hour to reach the fishing grounds, cruising at around 18 knots. It doesn't matter if it's sunny, overcast or raining. Gaetan has caught sharks in all conditions.

"It's not like fresh water fishing where if it's overcast and cloudy it would be better fishing than a sunny day," he says.

Perfect conditions include the absence of fog and just a bit of wind to encourage a slight drift but not so much so that it will cause clients discomfort.

Although the majority of fish landed are blue shark, later in the summer, when the water temperature rises, there's the opportunity to catch other species, including shortfin mako. Clients might hook up with them anywhere from one to six or seven times in the run of a season.

Gaetan used to start fishing the first week in July. But with global warming, water temperatures are rising faster and the season can stretch from the middle of June to the first week of October. He looks for a minimum temperature of 52 degrees Fahrenheit (10 or 11 degrees Celsius.) The water is warmer further from shore, a fact that surprises many.

"Everyone thinks the water is warmer inside and colder outside, but it's the opposite. The Gulf Stream has a lot to do with it," says Gaetan.

Hooks are removed from each shark's mouth before it is released. All fish caught are tagged, measured and photographed. There are dozens of photos of jubilant clients on his Blue Shark Fishing website.

"Basically the fish goes back to the water the same way it has come to me and in a lot of cases it's usually in better condition.

39

Friends provide encouragement. Photo courtesy Art Gaetan

"People have a tendency when they hold the fish to squeeze it because their adrenaline is pumping. You really can't squeeze them too much."

Gaetan collaborated with Dalhousie University on a paper about the catching and releasing of sharks in tournaments, to help educate fishermen on how to handle them once they get them to the side of the boat.

"I know for a fact that a lot of them bring them in, they're bouncing them around the deck, they're standing on them to pull the hook out of their mouth.... they're not really being treated very well, you know what I mean?

"I pull out anywhere between 100-150 long-line hooks every year from sharks that we catch. We catch them and one might have three long-line hooks in its mouth," he says.

Clients are taught about shark anatomy and learn about the nictitating membranes – a transparent third eyelid that can be drawn across the eye for protection and to moisten it while maintaining visibility. They also learn that sharks are like human beings in that they have a tendency to build up lactic acid in their bodies when they start getting tired.

"Lactic acid will kill the fish if you don't swim them properly to get rid of it. One way of checking for that is by their nictitating membranes.

"We explain all that when we bring the fish on board. It's an educational experience along with a fishing experience along with a nature tour," says Gaetan.

On some trips they've seen leatherback turtles that are drawn to the area to eat jellyfish. It's not unusual to see an ocean sunfish.

All may be serene and peaceful... until a shark strikes. Sharks are just like human beings, he says. They all have their own personality.

It's not uncommon for some species of shark to
"throw their stomach up" during landing.

"A six-foot shark might come up and take your bait and you won't even really know it until you see a fish swimming near the boat with a leader hanging out of his mouth. You might look down and say, 'Wow, look at that, he has a leader in his mouth.'

"Other ones will come in and they will literally almost destroy the rod, bouncing it around in the rod holder. They hit with such force," says Gaetan.

He teaches clients that sharks do not have any bones in their body and refers to them, paradoxically, as one of the most sensitive fish in the ocean. He says that 85 per cent of their "innards" is liver and reminds clients to be careful handling their shark once it is landed.

One of the sharks he tagged off of Halifax was recaptured 4,780 miles away in the South Atlantic. To his knowledge, it's the longest distance for a shark to be recaptured. What was also impressive about that specific fish is that it had inverted its stomach.

"When some sharks get nervous they'll 'throw their stomach up' and it looks like a great big chunk of liver," described Gaetan.

"It's actually hanging out of their mouth. People say that you can just take the hook out of their mouth and throw them back in and they'll swallow their stomach but I don't do that."

He's spent as long as 45 minutes making a shark swallow its stomach by putting a hose in its mouth so it can breath, then making it swallow the organ. When he and his crew captured the long-distance swimmer and reinserted the stomach he recorded the incident in his logbook.

When a fish is tagged then recaptured, the original tagger is provided with that information. The length of time that the shark was at sea from being tagged is always interesting.

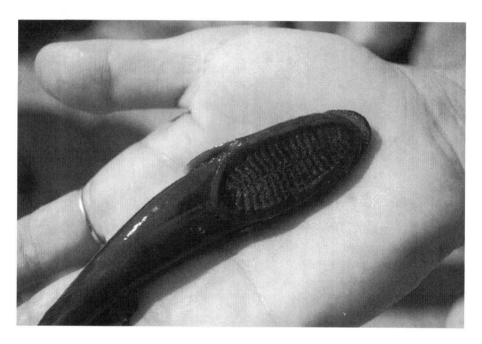

Remoras attach to some sharks and live off bacteria and other parasites on the host as well as food that floats free during eating.

From the figure he was provided, Gaetan determined that the fish swam an average of 21 miles a day to get to where it was recaptured.

"That's a fascinating number to be truthful with you," he says.

There are countless things about being at sea that are fascinating. Over his time on the ocean he's witnessed many incredible events.

"When you go out there, day in and day out, day in and day out, you're bound to bump into the odd freak of nature," he says.

On one occasion they tracked and followed two killer whales (orcas) that were swimming along the coast. Gaetan realized they were following a mother fin whale and her pup.

He described the diabolical plan that may have been behind their interest.

"Orcas will follow a mother whale and its pup for up to a number of weeks. What they try to do is separate the baby from its mother. When they do that they'll go on top of the baby and won't allow it to come to the surface. They actually drown the baby whale. Then the only thing they eat is the tongue of the whale.

"We saw a couple of orcas. There are two types of killer whales - resident whales that are usually in pods of six, or eight, or 10. They're a relatively safe breed. It's the transient killers, the outcasts from the pods that are the danger. When they swim together in two and three, they hunt. They can be very aggressive and they are one of the most intelligent animals in the ocean. We followed them for about an hour."

Another memorable experience was the whale shark sighting. It made him speechless. He added that there are not many things in this world that can do that. The whale shark was longer than the 34-foot boat they were in. There are few cases of whale shark being spotted as far North as Nova Scotia. This slow-moving, filter feeding shark mates and gives birth off Mexico.

Art Gaetan says he caught a mako shark larger than the
1,082-pound mako landed during the 2004 Shark Scramble.
"We had it estimated between 1,400 and 1,600 pounds.
She was bigger around than a 45-gallon drum," he said.
Photo courtesy Denis Gervais

Whale sharks have a lifespan of 70 years.

More tropical fish are being observed during fishing excursions. Gaetan caught a Queen triggerfish four or five years ago and he says they are starting to see more remora attached to some sharks. Also known as sharksuckers, these one-to-three-feet-long fish live off bacteria and other parasites on the host as well as food that floats free during eating.

He's also seen at least four great white sharks over his time at sea... but never actually caught one. The largest was estimated to be 16 or 17 feet long.

Gaetan says they even caught a mako shark that was larger than the famous one in Yarmouth. He believes it was even bigger than the world record shortfin mako (1,221 pounds) that was caught off Chatham, Mass. on July 21, 2001 by Luke Sweeney during the Oak Bluffs Monster Shark Tournament, from a 24-foot World Cat, the smallest boat in the tournament.

He says he's built his business on success and honesty, and that the following is no fish tale.

"That Yarmouth shark that they caught was only 1,082 pounds and that picture has travelled across the globe 10 times over. It's kind of funny how news travel around about something like that.

"But we caught a mako shark out here about six years ago and we had it estimated between 1,400 and 1,600 pounds. It looked like it was carrying pups - 11 feet long but she had a girth of between seven and eight feet. She was bigger around than a 45-gallon drum. It took us six hours to get her to the side of the boat and once we got her to the side of the boat she was completely exhausted and full of lactic acid. We swam her for the better part of an hour and 20 minutes before I felt comfortable enough to let her go. When we did she kicked her tail up and swam off. It was a good feeling and there was high-fiving in the boat.

Note the balloon on the end of the pole. Conservationists recommend other floats. When sharks strike, they snap the balloon. It floats free and is sometimes mistaken as a jellyfish and eaten by a leatherback turtle or ocean sunfish, which then dies.

"No one ever hears of the large fish we catch because in order to claim that fish I would have had to kill it. You take a gene pool like that out of the ocean... there's not a whole lot of those ones left. To kill a fish like that just to put your name in a book is really sad."

One of the more unusual methods of fishing for shark is by fly. Although he says he's not a fly fisherman "by any stretch of the imagination" he can do the job and get the thing out.

"Most people think you use these huge, monster flies. But you use a salmon fly. We use a stainless steel hook versus an iron hook because it's a little stronger. You can apply a little more pressure to the fish with a salt-water hook than a regular hook. It's amazing really the amount of pressure you can put on a fish with a fly rod.

"What's really cool with the fly rod is that blue sharks, a lot of the times when you put a lot of pressure on their mouths, they have a tendency of rolling up into the leader. That causes two problems: if he rolls past your leader and up into your line his skin sometimes will cut the line and then you leave the shark swimming around with a bunch of line hanging off him, which is not very cool.

"But it's rare that that happens with the fly rod because you don't apply enough pressure that they want to roll so when the fish comes to the side of the boat you have the hook in the perfect side in the corner of their mouth. it's a good feeling. We bring him up onboard and pop the hook out of his mouth."

Blue Shark Fishing Charters use all barbless hooks. Gaetan has trialed circle hooks because they are recommended for catch-and-release fishing but he's not impressed. He's had "gut hooks" with circle hooks that have really put him off. He's not convinced that circle hooks are the way to go for shark fishing.

During a fishing trip, he will likely share his pet peeve with you - the practice of using balloons for fishing floats.

49

From left to right: Rick (first mate, Zach's father); Captain Art and Casey, the shark hunting dog; Elaina (aka Lynn, Art's wife); Michelle and Mike (close friends of Art and Elaina). Photo courtesy of Art Gaetan

When sharks strike, they snap the balloon and it floats free, only to often to be mistaken as a jellyfish and consumed by a leatherback turtle or ocean sunfish, which can then die.

"I've been trying to get rid of those damn balloon things for the past 10 years or so. There's no need of using them. There's a float product that slides up and down your line and if you happen to inadvertently hook a fast-moving species like a bluefin tuna, mako or huge blue (shark), the float will actually give an indication as to which way the fish is on the move. Balloons for me are like the taboo of the taboos when they go on the water. They're really nasty, nasty," he says.

He condemns the practice of releasing balloons during special celebrations because of the great distance they can travel - in some cases up to 5,000 kilometres before they reach the stratosphere and currents snatch them. He points out that 95 per cent of all the air currents circulating the planet go over oceans. Chances are high that those balloons will end up over the sea and the heating and cooling of that large body of water will suck them down. He and his crew have recovered balloons off Halifax that were released in Florida.

Another conservation measure he'd like to see put into place is the practice of catch-and-release by the organizers of Nova Scotia's shark fishing tournaments. He points out that for the past 10 or 12 years, Americans have been doing this.

He's suggested it to the Yarmouth Shark Scramble committee but they've come back with reasons for maintaining the status quo.

"Their concern is that people are paying big money to bring a fish in and the public wants to see a fish. Okay, you can bring in a fish but you don't have to bring in 40 or 50 fish. A shark is a shark is a shark," he says.

He concedes that leaps and bounds have been made in protecting sharks – primarily the increase in length for allowable catches from six to eight feet.

51

The catch and release method of shark fishing helps
to protect the marine food chain. Photo courtesy of Art Gaetan

Fishermen bring back exciting memories and impressive fishing
tales after an excursion with Art Gaetan, instead of dead sharks.
Photo courtesy of Art Gaetan

He also stresses that he's in favour of the derbies because it's the only time for scientists to "get into the guts" of sharks to find out what's actually going on with these animals.

"But you don't have to kill every one. Catch-and-release tournaments would allow you to limit the number of sharks that you actually would take in but then you'd have to have an observer on board or someone that's honest on every boat. They're a little reluctant to change at this point but I believe in the future they're not going to have any choice in the matter. There's a lot of public pressure right now on the decline in the world's shark population.

"What the general public has no idea of is that when our sharks are gone, life on our planet could very well come to a halt. We get 75 per cent of our oxygen from the oceans of the world and the top predator of the ocean is the shark. He keeps it all in balance. If you take that guy out that balances the ocean, the food chain will reverse itself.

"You'll get to a point where you eliminate all of the phytoplankton in the ocean that makes the oxygen. Once that 75 per cent is gone we'll have to rely on 25 per cent from all of our trees and forests. As we know, the rain forests are in trouble as well. It's not going to be a happy place here in another 50 to 100 years.

"I love sharks. They're an amazing creature. I don't care if I ever catch another shark. For me it's the satisfaction of taking people out. If you look at my photos, 90 per cent are of their faces. It's the pleasure that you bring. When you see grown men crying on the boat from excitement, to me that brings joy."

Type in shark fishing as a search on Google and Blue Shark Fishing Charters is number one. The site receives anywhere between 5,000 and 8,000 hits a month. It's located at: www.bluesharkcharters.com

A shark is lowered to the dock after weighing.

Chapter 5 - Let the reel rip

Reprinted with permission from The Yarmouth Vanguard

Jeff Gamble says he was thankful that the 402-pound thresher shark with the 10-foot tail they hauled aboard the *Costalot* was exhausted after its fight with the rod.

"If he had started whipping that thing around the boat everyone would have been diving," he said.

At sea, the shark uses its large caudal fin to slap the water, forcing schools of herring, mackerel and cephalopods like squid into tighter schools so the tail can be whipped to stun and/or kill them. They've also been known to kill sea birds with their tails.

Gamble, along with John Gould, Don Sampson and Paul Moase, came from Toronto for the Yarmouth Shark Scramble. They learned of it through Joan Moyer, an associate of Gould's. Moyer's sister Ginny is married to Jim Hurlburt, captain of the *Costalot*, which is owned by Bruce and Doreen Nickerson. This was Gamble's second shark fishing expedition. His first was off New York.

"It wasn't nearly as exciting as this one. Not even close," said Gamble.

He says what made the Yarmouth Shark Scramble so exciting was the way the sharks were caught – off a lobster fishing boat, using stand-up gear as opposed to sitting in a chair aboard a sports fishing boat.

During the two hours and 10 minutes it took to land the big fish, everybody took turns with the rod, with Hurlburt coaching.

"He never left the side of whoever was fishing, which was amazing," said Gamble.

A picture to remember.

The crew didn't see much of the thresher during the fight.

"It was so far down. If it got any kind of glimpse of the boat it would just go straight down.

"One guy would make some headway and hand the reel off to another guy and it would just rip off 150 to 200 yards and then we'd have to re-do it all over again," said Gamble.

Near the end, the crew was fighting fatigue as much as the shark.

"It got to a point where someone would say, 'Who's next? And no-body was putting their hand up.'

"It's very strenuous on your lower back. When I first took the rod I had it for nearly 30 minutes and then every other shift after that it wasn't for more than five minutes," said Gamble.

He says when the thresher finally came to the surface, he wasn't thrashing around like some of the other sharks they'd landed.

The crew put another hook in the jaw and a noose around his belly to make it easier to haul it aboard the boat. Their shark won the tournament.

A 201 lb. blue shark and 221 lb. mako shark were landed in addition to several small blues that were tagged and released.

Gamble and his friends say they enjoyed the experience immensely and have the event well documented. Crews on neighbouring boats told of seeing someone climbing in *Costalot's* rigging while at sea.

"That was me," said Gamble, laughing.
"I needed better angles for the video camera."

The fishermen hoped to return again, likely with others.

"We were challenged," said Gamble.

"When they gave me the trophy, they invited us back, so we will be back."

Shark Scramble fame continues to draw participants from afar, including New York, Nunavut, Maine, New Brunswick and North Carolina.

Dr. Steven Campana, senior scientist at the
Bedford Institute of Oceanography,
and the head of the Canadian Shark Research Laboratory.
(Photo credit: Dr. Steven Campana, Bedford Institute of Oceanography, Canada)

Chapter 6 - Shark Research

Millions of sharks visit the waters off the Atlantic provinces annually. Some of these weigh hundreds of pounds and can reach lengths of 10 to 15 feet.

Sharks may be the apex predator in the ocean but mankind poses a serious threat to their survival. The commercial long-line fishery kills thousands of tons of sharks as bycatch when they are inadvertently caught with tuna and swordfish. Recreational shark fishing and derbies, though viewed unfavourably by some, actually pose less of a problem and benefit scientists with the valuable information they provide.

Shark fishing derbies in the province are not organized by the Canadian Shark Research Laboratory (CSRL) at the Bedford Institute of Oceanography. The lab is responsible for research and stock assessment of the shark species found off of the eastern coast of Canada, particularly those that are fished commercially or recreationally. Dr. Steven Campana, senior scientist at BIO and head of the CSRL, says the shark fishing events are a community driven exercise.

"They do get approval by the fisheries' managers and DFO Science, which is us. We take full advantage of all the information we can get. That part of it has turned out to be pretty useful."

Scientists collect useful scientific data during the events, including the length, weight and sexual maturity of sharks. They also examine   stomach contents. Trends in this data are monitored, in addition to other information supplied by the shark derbies. From this, changes in the population level can be determined, which can be an indication of low stocks or overfishing.

Shark technician Warren Joyce holds a freshly cut shark jaw.

In a 2004 research document, *Influence of Recreational and Commercial Fishing on the Blue Shark (Prionace Glauca) Population in Atlantic Canadian Waters* by Campana, S.E., Marks, L., Joyce, W., and Kohler, N., it was determined that shark tournaments only account for about three per cent of the blue shark fishing mortality in Canadian waters.

Thus the tournaments are having a negligible effect on population abundance and overall mortality.

"It is a drop in the bucket," said Campana.

He added that the events have turned out to be a good way for scientists to monitor the health of the population simply because the large number of blue sharks that are caught in the commercial fishery tend to be discarded.

Scientific technicians and observers on long-liners reported these vessels accidentally catch very large numbers of blue sharks with almost 100 per cent being thrown back. Roughly 2/3 of the blue sharks that are caught in commercial longlining operations survive all stages of the fishing and release process. In the Canadian Atlantic, the unreported bycatch of blue sharks is estimated to be many times larger than the reported catch.

Research has shown that the weight of sharks landed at recreational shark tournaments has increased from around four metric tons in 1993 to around 20 metric tons in recent years. Blue sharks accounted for 99 per cent of all sharks landed. The recreational catch-and-release fishery catches another 13 mt annually.

Data from past tournaments showed that mature females were not present in the catches. However, the size composition at the derbies was not representative of the population: small sharks were poorly represented (due to derby catch restrictions) and large males were over-represented (due to their being targeted by derby participants).

Dr. Steven Campana measures a shark before it is dissected.

The absence of mature female sharks from the catches was one of the biggest finds for scientists studying derby data. Campana commented on the abnormality.

"It's very unusual. I can't think of very many, if any, other fish species where we don't have at least some mature females in our waters. This is something that probably would have been pretty hard to pick up based on just sampling the commercial catches," he said.

The lack of females is viewed as a very fortuitous event. It means the most important and vulnerable part of the population, the spawning females, are not around to be caught.

Since the initial data was supplied, the mystery of where the mature females are appears to have been solved.

"When we look at the reports of what the Spanish and the Portuguese are catching over on the eastern side of the Atlantic, they have a lot of big females there. We don't know where they mate and go to give birth," said Campana.

Scientists have examined the trends in Canadian waters over the years and the blue shark population has remained at a reasonably high level with perhaps a slight decline over the years.

However, only a part of the population can be observed, as blue sharks are highly migratory, swimming literally all over the Atlantic.

Researchers have determined from tagging that blue sharks that are off our coast one month can be in the middle of the Atlantic, off South America, or sometimes off the European or African coast, three or four months later.

Scientists have determined that the blue shark population has
remained at a reasonably high level with perhaps
a slight decline over the years.

ICCAT (The International Commission for the Conservation of Atlantic Tunas) is the organization that's primarily responsible for tuna and swordfish in the Atlantic. It also monitors the shark population.

"They tried a couple of times to do a blue shark assessment but the data is really poor, simply because most countries throw them back. They don't want them, and they tend not to keep good records on them," said Campana.

The ICCAT's last assessment suggested that blue sharks are in excellent condition and there was no apparent downturn at all. Most people don't entirely believe that, simply because they're caught in such huge numbers every year. There must be some impact on the population (thinks the general public) but trying to find the numbers to back that up is hard.

One factor in the blue shark's favour is that it is a healthy propagator. Females give birth to pups after a gestation period of between nine and 12 months. Litters can consist of 25 to 50. The newborns measure 40 to 51 cm in length. An interesting oddity is that after copulation the females can retain and nourish the spermatozoa in the oviducal gland for months or years while awaiting ovulation.

The practice of tagging sharks has provided fascinating data to scientists. There are two types of tags. Catch-and-release charter operations and derby fishermen put on the more conventional tags that are similar in appearance to sphagetti - thin pieces of coloured plastic with return information on them.

"We've had approximately 30 of those recaptured over the last few years. A lot of the recaptures are being made by Spanish fishermen out in the middle of the Atlantic Ocean," said Campana.

The more expensive satellite tagging ($4,000/unit) is generally performed by BIO staff. Scientists receive data on where the shark goes, how deep it swims and the water temperature.

Chris Brown holds up scraps of seal
removed from a shark's stomach.

"We never have to get the shark back because the tag physically releases from the shark, reports back to a satellite and then back to us. We've got another 40 or 50 of these satellite tags to put on over the next couple of years," said Campana.

In 2011, the research paper: *Migration Pathways, Behavioural Thermoregulation and Overwintering Grounds of Blue Sharks in the Northwest Atlantic,* by Campana, Anna Dorey, Mark Fowler, Warren Joyce, Zeliang Wang, Dan Wright, Igor Yashayaev, was published.

A random sampling of 40 sharks was tagged with wildlife computers pop-up archival transmitting tags (PATs). All but two of the sharks were sexually immature. Tagged sharks were on deck an average of three minutes for tagging and measurement and showed no obvious injury from the experience.

The sharks were tagged by darting a nylon umbrella tip near the dorsal fin using a monofilament leader of 400-pound test, sheathed to reduce trauma. Each PAT was also fitted with an emergency cutoff device provided by the manufacturer that releases the tag if it goes below 1800 metres.

The PATs record depth, temperature and light intensity at one-minute or 10-second intervals, depending on the model, for a period of two to six months after release.

Around 92 per cent of the tags transmitted successfully after release from the shark. All of the PATs were programmed to release from the fish if a constant depth was maintained for four days, since a continued presence on the ocean floor would mean the shark had died.

Shark location at the time of pop-up was determined with an accuracy of one kilometre through Doppler-shift calculations provided by the Argos satellite data collection and location service.

A gory job.

From the transmitted data, scientists learned that all of the blue sharks moved off the continental shelf to the south and/or east after tagging. Most sharks were north of latitude 30uN at the time of pop-up, although one travelled more than 2500 km to the southeast of Cuba (21uN). The distance travelled ranged between 141 and 2566 km.

Over the following months it was noted that most sharks remained near the warm waters of the Gulf Stream, or the Sargasso Sea, which is farther south.

An interesting phenomenon was the tendency of blue sharks to dive very deeply (200 m) during the daytime once they reached the Gulf Stream. They stayed deep throughout their daytime stay there, or in the Sargasso Sea, returning to surface waters each night. The initiation of the deep diving behaviour was so characteristic of entering the Gulf Stream that it could be used as an entry diagnostic by itself.

At that depth, the water temperature declines from around 18 degrees Celsius to 15. When surface temperatures were warm, the sharks appeared to dive deeper. The moon had an effect on their diving depth as well. Brighter surface waters appeared to drive the sharks deeper. During full moon they went three times deeper compared to new moons.

Scientists initially formed several hypotheses to explain the daily pattern of deep diving in blue sharks. These included the possibility that they may be foraging for food, regulating their body temperature, taking advantage of depth-related variations in currents, mating, avoiding predators, or navigating.

Because all but two of the tagged sharks were sexually immature, the explanation of reproduction was doubtful. As sharks are at the top of the food chain, predator avoidance was also unlikely.

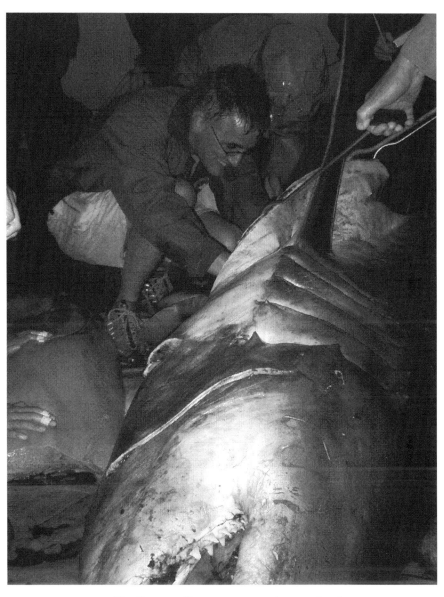

Dr. Steven Campana examines a shark
during the Yarmouth Shark Scramble.

The best explanation was that the sharks stay deep to feed. However, they appear to be functionally blind where they spend their daytime hours at those depths.

Campana says they are continuing to see the deep diving behaviour exhibited with the new tags that are deployed. The feeding hypothesis and thermoregulation theory are becoming more accepted.

"Right now we're fairly convinced it's a combination of the foraging, chasing their squid prey in particular, up and down, but also thermo-regulation. The idea that the surface waters of the Gulf Stream are so hot that if the sharks hang out up there in the daytime when there's no food around, they burn off more energy than if they swim down deep and don't even feed because it's cooler down below of course.

"It's a combination of the two. We really only see that yo-yo type diving in the blue sharks. All of the tags we've put on the porbeagle, for instance, they don't do the same type of things at all. As a matter of fact because they like cooler water than the blue shark, they tend to literally dive underneath the Gulf Stream when they're swimming down to the Sargasso Sea to give birth."

Studies showed that the young blue sharks from the northern sector of the northwest Atlantic overwinter close to six months in the warm off-shore waters.

U.S. tagging data provided similar results, with 92 per cent of blue sharks tagged in the northwest Atlantic being recaptured in the north-west Atlantic, and only four per cent migrating across the Atlantic.

Extensive conventional tagging data off Ireland delivered almost a mirror image of the northwest Atlantic movements.

A crescent-shaped jawline conceals rows of jagged teeth.

The sharks moved to the west and southwest from Europe and they overwintered in the central and offshore east Atlantic.

The overall tagging results point to the north central Atlantic as being a major overwintering ground for immature blue sharks from all areas of the north Atlantic.

The dissections of blue sharks and other species that are performed by BIO staff at annual shark tournaments have provided additional information.

There are two things that scientists are specifically looking for while performing these. Sexual maturity is of interest and continues to be monitored. This can be determined in male sharks by observing the condition of their claspers, the penis-like organs that hang down from the base of the pelvic fins.

The females must be examined internally to observe the size of their uterus and eggs. That's how biologists have been able to determine there are no sexually mature females in our waters.

Stomach contents are examined to determine what sharks are eating. Campana says blue sharks are not exactly picky eaters.

"Most of their diet is fish and squid, but there's a lot of garbage that's in there - plastic bags, lobster bands and plastic bands. We had one stomach that had not one, but two different types of beer cans in it. They're not very discriminatory. We also get the more interesting stuff, pieces of seal and dolphin and the occasional seabird.

"Once a shark gets big, it's pretty tough. A small blue shark could easily be eaten by a different type of shark and we see that on occasion.

"But once a shark gets past its juvenile stage, they're pretty much the king of the food web," he said.

One of Campana's students recently finished a project that examines the mating habits of blue sharks. The student determined that male blue sharks, as part of their mating behaviour, will actually bite and grip the female to hold it in position while it attempts to mate. Very often, female blue sharks are landed at derbies and elsewhere in the commercial catch with half-moon-shaped tooth imprints on them.

"We know from measurements over the years how big the jaw is in the male blue shark, as it gets bigger, its jaw gets bigger. We can measure the diameter of the bite marks on the females and reconstruct how big the male was that was attempting to mate with her.

"What we've found is that a lot of the females that are showing up with these bite marks are immature. They're not even capable of pregnancy. But the males are going after them anyways and when we reconstruct the size we see that it's not just the newbie males that are inexperienced. Sometimes it's the really big males as well," said Campana.

He refers to mankind as custodians of sharks and believes it's easier to protect something once you know what it's doing. With the assistance of fishermen at derbies and on recreational fishing charters, information gathering has broadened.

Campana is co-authoring a book to be released in 2013. *Sharks in Canada* will include a collection of photos and fascinating anecdotes as well as field guide information.

For an authoritative and comprehensive site on sharks in Canada, visit the Canadian Shark Research Laboratory website at www.marinebiodiversity.ca/shark

This 1,082-pound mako, caught during the 2004
Yarmouth Shark Scramble, turned into an urban legend.

Chapter 7 - Birth of an Urban Legend

Amongst all the blood, gore and guts of the 2004 Yarmouth Shark Scramble I snagged a shot that drove home the importance of copyright. A 10-foot, 10-inch, 1082-pound mako shark was caught by Jamie Doucette aboard the Pembroke Princess. I got down low in front and snapped it from the jaw, filed the photo for our paper and then the fun began.

It's hard to say where the first snatching incident occurred (my guess is off the now defunct Halifax Daily News website) but from there that picture circulated like wildfire. Friends sent it to friends who sent it to friends. The actual location of the catch was lost in cyberspace. It wasn't important apparently. Neither was the name of the angler or photographer. And the description of the catch... well... you know how fishing tales grow!

G.J. LeBlanc, owner of The Magazine Yarmouth website, says he was amazed that misinformation could spread that far.

"People like fish tales. It's a practical joke. They got it and they just changed the name and sent it to a friend. The key thing that most people pointed out in their responses was the area code on the side of the forklift. That's what tipped them off to the real location."

He was also impressed by how many people wrote comments about the photo on his site.

"The number of people that actually took the time to look it up or make a comment is only one in a thousand (that likely viewed the photo). It was all over the place. Jaws. People are terrified of sharks," he concluded.

The urban legend was eventually posted to Snopes.com, which stated that claims of a half-ton shark being caught in Yarmouth, Nova Scotia, were true.

A nasty-looking set of choppers stands in the way of hook removal.

Charles Duhigg wrote a story for the Los Angeles Times (Nov. 2, 2004), entitled *Epic Mako Loses Shark Brawl in the Atlantic*. Candus Thomson wrote *Fishy Shark Tale Holds No Water* for the Baltimore Sun (March 9, 2008). The Vancouver Sun published *Shark Capture is quite the fish story* on June 21, 2008.

The following collection of comments are from hundreds on LeBlanc's website (www.yarmouth.org/magazine/urban.htm). They provide a good sampling of the silliness.

The place names associated with the picture in the beginning were Barkley Sound in British Columbia, and Ocean Shores, Washington. "Don't Go Swimming In Barkley Sound" was a popular header. The mako became a great white shark in some accounts and the true name of the boat - *Pembroke Princess* - became *Dawn Raider*. One tall tale that was forwarded repeatedly, said the boat was fishing dogfish commercially when it hooked the "great white" in the mouth.

"It only resisted slightly for 15 minutes before it came up alongside the boat to have a look; long enough for one of the crew members to slip a rope around its tail! And that's when the s**t hit the fan! The shark took off towing the 42-foot fishing boat backwards through the water at about seven knots. Just like in Jaws, the boat was taking on water over the stern and the crew watched in horror as the shark would actually jump completely out of the water at times. This went on for an hour before the shark finally drowned."

In 2004

From Victoria, BC

I received this same message through government sources, both federal and provincial (BC), and though the telephone number on the lift is a Nova Scotian number, it isn't entirely out of place to find a great white on the west coast. It also didn't seem out of place to find equipment produced on the east coast but possibly used on both coasts nor is the fog identifiable as east coast fog v/s west coast fog. Port Albion is a legitimate port, across the bay from Uclelet in Barkley Sound, and did not raise any flags.

A biologist takes the measurements of a massive shark.

Our biggest clue that this might be a hoax is that it certainly would have made the local news and none of our acquaintances, many who fish or dive on the west coast, had heard anything about this occurrence. Gotta love a good story!

From Quadra Island, BC
Prior to moving to Quadra Island I was a fisheries observer in the area that the aforementioned critter was reported to be caught. Having been on all of the docks in that area at one time or another, the dock in the picture didn't look familiar unless someone had done a major overhaul in the recent past. The rest of the story seemed very plausible though. We even went so far as to call some friends who are still in the area to see if they'd heard anything about it. Good joke and my hat's off to the creator.

From Yellowknife, NT
I received the email in Yellowknife, from my brother in Victoria, BC. I have heard of great whites being caught off the west coast in Canada before, so I partially believed it. But I looked for a news article about it on the web, and found this site instead.

From BC
I just dragged my brother in here to look at it. I fear sharks...fear them… and to know they were off the coast scared the bejesus outta me. Glad to know it was not here!

From Cape Town, South Africa
It was posted onto yahoogroups surfski newsgroup this morning... My email hoax antennae started quivering even though it didn't have the "send this to all your friends" phrase that signals the usual email hoax...

In 2005

From Winnipeg, MB
Received a copy of the myth from my brother who lives in Thailand. The story is going around the globe.
Cheers

There's a mixture of expressions in the crowd
as this giant shark is hoisted high on the forklift.

From Calgary, AB
This myth freaked out my girlfriend... we had surfed in Ucluelet this summer... she is desperately afraid of sharks.

From Oregon
Got it from a former boss in Sitka, Alaska.

From Madisonville, Texas
I have received this email twice. Scary looking shark I must say!

From Vancouver, BC
My uncle sent me this from France! (He is from Vancouver too). Thanks.

From Leeds, West Yorkshire, UK
Hook, line and sinker - you had me fooled, ye gits! Like an eejit I went and forwarded it to The South Africa White Shark Research Institute, of which I'm a member. Now I'll have to retract. So they'll know I'm an eejit too.

From Boston, MA
Received from a friend in Seattle where it supposedly happened.

From Corvallis, Oregon
Just got the email. This time it claimed the shark was caught outside of Gray's Harbor in Washington state.

From Chemanius, BC
By saying that the fish was caught in Barkley Sound, all we had had was some jerk trying to scare tourists away from the West Coast and ruin the local tourism economy. After seeing "Jaws" a few times gullible American tourists tend to get pretty nervous when they see those kinds of pictures and they might just be put off on that kayaking or fishing holiday in Canada.... or go to Alaska where they know the water is too cold for Great Whites.

Competition for tourism dollars is fierce, it's a lucrative business, and I wouldn't put it past any "out of area" operator to post such pictures to spread fear and misinformation in order to create uncertainty about a visitor's safety.

A biologist measures the teeth and jaw
of a tournament shark.

Tourism is fickle and it doesn't take much to ruin the industry.... just look at what SARS did to tourism... which was for the most part a no show. Just the media hype was all it took.

Hoaxes are not funny...

From Yarmouth, NS
Wow...It's amazing how stories get so twisted. A funny thing is that my sister married a Calgarian this summer, during the time of the shark scramble. A lot of his family and friends all came down for the wedding. Those pictures look a lot like the pictures that his uncle took, while he was down here...but then again, a lot of people were snapping pictures when that shark was caught! Interesting...maybe when they visit Calgary this summer they will tell the real story.

From Annapolis Valley, NS
I'm from Annapolis Valley, NS, and would like to thank those responsible for correcting the false information on an awesome Atlantic predator. First off, although we do have great whites off all the coast lines around Nova Scotia in mid to late summer (considered rare though), the shark pictured (probably caught off the southwestern part of the province) is not a great white at all, its a short-fin mako. I have to agree with the bottom statement on the catch being almost a shame seeing as how she is obviously successful at surviving to attain such a large adult length.

From White Rock, BC
I received this email from a friend that works in the wholesale fishing industry. The story was still being passed around at 11:30 a.m. Thursday. I just sent this to them and I'm sure that they will have a good chuckle. They probably already had visions of cashing in on shark orders.

From San Diego, CA
Haha...this was a good one. Entertaining, even though it was fake. Still a huge shark! Wow.

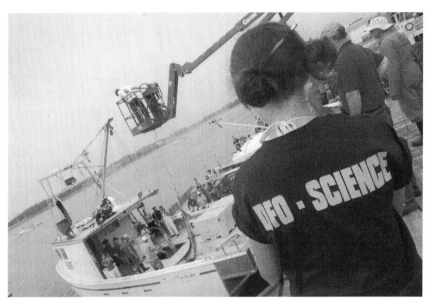

Department of Fisheries and Oceans
scientists monitor the shark catch.

In 2006

From Sweden
As a former Island resident, I was intrigued upon receiving the email,
but alas it is from the right coast! Is funny how long this has been
going around and I'm sure some will continue to be from Ukke for
years to come! Good on y'all!

In 2007

From Cle Elum, Washington
This photo was just brought into our meat market here in Cle Elum,
Wa. (Owens Meats) by a local who does underwater log recovery. He
told us that this shark was caught up in some hooks and cable line
from a commercial fisherman and he responded to a radio call and
asked for his help. Jim Smith told us that he responded and hoisted
the fish onto his boat with a cable wrapped around its head up the
ramp of his old naval torpedo recovery boat, which is 70 feet long and
that while it was being drug up the ramp it was rocking his boat as the
shark was going crazy just prior to dying.

Jim pointed out that it was him standing next to the shark on the dock,
which honestly looked just like him.

This all happened inside Grays Harbor by West Port Washington. Jim
told us that the shark was a great white and measured 15 feet long. We
enjoyed the story until coming across your web page.

From Elko, Nevada
I am a fisherwoman and a shark lover and wanted to know a little more
about the story so I googled and your site came up. I know nothing
about the areas they were talking about so nothing about the towns
really tipped me off that this was a gag. The story itself warranted more
investigation. It goes to show you can't believe everything you read on
the Internet. I'd sure like to know the real fishing story (are there real
fishing stories?) that involved that shark. I bet it was a blast!

Fishermen relax once back in port, awaiting
a turn at the scale with their sharks.

From Yarmouth, NS

I am the captain of the boat *Pembroke Princess* "who caught the shark" three years ago, in Yarmouth Nova Scotia , Canada.

Jamie was my son in law. I'm amazed at how this shark has traveled the Internet world wide, and how people will take something like this and twist the stories and pictures around to their advantage. We, the crew, have the real story, on board, pictures never seen…

IF it wasn't for our whole crew, there wouldn't be the shark, **our shark.**

Bernard Tedford

From Seattle, Washington

Got the Westport Washington hoax story on "Great White Shark." Of course I passed it on to mariner friends on NW N America coast. Within about 6 hours, I received information from a friend that I had been taken in. Great stories become world wide myths in hours in to-day's world…… and it looks like they keep coming back up for another round of suckers to enjoy.

Regards,

Ron Parypa,

m/v Rhapsody

In 2008

From Western Australia

I also received the massive shark story even now in 2008!

The story was changed to say that the shark was caught off Rottnest Island in Western Australia, (a hugely popular swimming spot). Straight away I googled the phone number on the crane. A number from Dartmouth, Nova Scotia, Canada came up. On further inspection of the 2nd photo you can see a Canadian flag on the mast of the fishing boat in the background!

Participants watch the proceedings carefully
to see if any other sharks weigh more than theirs.

From Perth, Australia

The shark email swam into my inbox today, 9th October, 2008. I googled the topic and here I am!

From Baltimore, MD

This came to me as a "great white" caught near the Chesapeake Bay Bridge near a park called Sandy Point. Sandy Point happens to be the park/beach where nearly 8,000 (+/-) people jump into the water (as they do every year) during the Polar Bear Plunge in January to raise funds for the Maryland Special Olympics.
Hey up there in Nova Scotia. :O)

From Annapolis, MD

Chesapeake Bay, near Route 50 Bay Bridge and Sandy Point State Park… at last I have the ultimate excuse not to do the Polar Bear Plunge in January. It's not only crazy to jump into freezing cold water, it could be downright dangerous! Note the expression on the face of the man wearing the red baseball cap. He's still scared half out of his wits and glad to be alive!

From Baltimore, MD

The email I received said that this shark was caught in the upper Chesapeake Bay near the bay bridge in Annapolis, MD. At first I thought, hey it could be possible considering we've had other animals wander into our bay like a sea-cow (Florida manatee)… but after I sent it to a few friends I slowly realized it couldn't be true. I thought it wouldn't be possible for a great white to survive in such low salinity levels considering they said it was caught in January when salinity levels are lower in the bay and in that location salinity doesn't get high enough during any part of the year for that kind of fish and even if it could survive our brackish waters what about the area code on the crane lifting it! Duhhh you big dummie!

John Boudreau pushes a shark into position for viewing.

In 2010

From Baltimore, MD
January 20, 2010: Just received the e-mail with pics attached, detailing the story of the landing of the great white. The version I received stated that the shark was caught in the Chesapeake Bay.

No names were used in the story, although the vessel "*Dawn Raider*" out of Markley's Marina in Essex, MD was noted.

Every January, the Polar Bear Plunge is held at Sandy Point State Park on the Chesapeake. Given the timing and the added caption of "Anyone signed up for the Polar Bear Plunge?", I'm sure someone in Maryland is having a good laugh. Special Olympics of Maryland, the beneficiary of the Plunge, may not find it so humorous.

From Grapeview, Washington
I have received this a few times this week AGAIN! Get it about two or three times a year. First time I got it, we were living in Hawaii!

I too did a reverse search on the phone number (that poor company, hope they got some good biz from all the folks who must have called!)

Aloha!

I'm going to save this website, this is pretty cool. I usually use About.com, but this was way more thorough on this story anyway! Great job!

In 2011

From Amsterdam, The Netherlands
I got this email from my brother and instantly thought, this can NOT be true! (Does that make me cynical and mistrusting? :-)). A quick search on Google turned up your page.

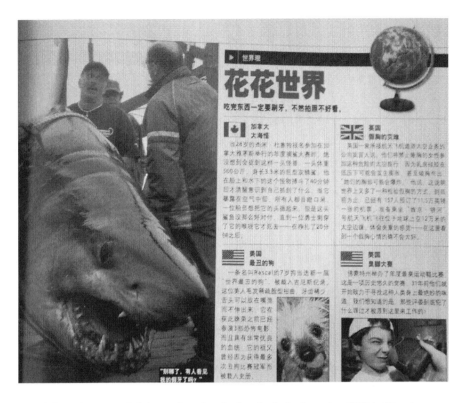

The picture of this mako shark, landed during the 2004 Shark Scramble in Yarmouth, was circulated around the world and ended up being published in an issue of Chinese Maxim.

Chapter 8 - Selling the Snap

I realized I had to start reclaiming my shark photo when contacted by the Los AngelesTimes for reprint rights. They paid me the princely sum of $150. After that I spent hours online googling the image, using the search words *Yarmouth Mako*, or its weight (1082-pound shark). The picture had been published on websites around the world. I sent an email to each webmaster, not asking them to take it off, only requesting they add my name as the photographer. All of them complied. The "free advertising" worked in my favour.

I continue to sell reprint rights in the years following. Markets have included Field & Stream, Maxim USA, Maxim China, Prank Patrol and most recently Dreamworks for part of the set design in Tropic Thunder.

The picture also won second place in the 2005 Canadian Community Newspaper Awards spot news photo competition.

A 1778 oil painting at the National Gallery of Art, Washington,
D.C., by John Singleton Copley, depicts a shark attack
that took place in Havana, Cuba, in 1749.
(Public domain photo)

Chapter 9 – Shark Attacks

Part of the fear and fascination that mankind has with sharks can be attributed to attacks that have occurred over the centuries. But what are the odds of actually being attacked by a shark? According to the University of Florida's International Shark Attack File (ISAF), the chance is one in 11.5 million.

More than 5,000 individual investigations are included in the file, which covers incidents occurring from the mid-1500s to today. The records are stored at the Florida Museum of Natural History on the university campus and managed by the American Elasmobranch Society, a professional organization comprised of international workers studying sharks, skates and rays.

The data is utilized by biological researchers and research physicians, but access is granted only after careful screening on a case-by-case basis. Access by the press and general public is strictly forbidden as there are concerns of sensationalism from improper use of photos, medical/autopsy reports, audio/video files and other sensitive material.

The Florida Program for Shark Research is involved in many areas of study, including shark biology, ecology, and behaviour. In addition, the FPSR monitors shark attacks through the file and promotes shark conservation and educational outreach through such programs as Project Shark Awareness.

The ISAF reports that the number of worldwide unprovoked shark attacks has grown at a steady pace since 1900, with each decade having more attacks than the previous one. However, the numerical growth in shark interactions does not necessarily mean that there is an increase in the rate of shark attacks.

Shark fishing tournaments draw spectators in all types of vessels.

It more likely reflects the ever-increasing amount of time spent in the sea by humans, which, in turn, increases the opportunities for interaction. The advent of the Internet also enables easier record sharing and communication.

Sharks do not normally hunt humans, says the National Oceanic and Atmospheric Administration Fisheries Service. When humans are attacked, it is usually a case of mistaken identity. Sharks can mistake humans for their natural prey, such as fish or a marine mammal or sea turtle. Most often it will release the person after the first bite.

The majority of shark bites are "hit-and-run" attacks by smaller species. They mistake thrashing arms or dangling feet as prey, dart in, bite and let go when they realize it's not a fish. The "big three" species -- bull, tiger and great white sharks --are big enough to do a lot of damage to a human and must be treated with respect and caution.

Although there has been no report of significant harm to anyone from shark attacks off the Canadian Atlantic provinces, there have been incidents.

The Canadian Shark Research Laboratory describes a 1932 incident in which a great white shark attacked a motor boat as a father and his son were hauling in fishing gear near Digby Gut, NS. During what must have been a terrifying experience, the shark bumped into the boat repeatedly, leaving several teeth in the hull and keel. From examining these, it was determined the shark was approximately 4.6 metres in length.

In the fall of 2000, a shark (suspected as being a porbeagle) showed unusual interest in a sea urchin diver off Digby. It could have been the nearby lobster bait that attracted the shark, which bumped the diver, tried to grab his catch bag and hauled him several feet before letting go. The shark circled the diver for a while afterwards.

In other areas of the world, shark attacks are more common.

A security guard opens the jaw of a shark to provide a closer look.

Travel & Leisure magazine culled data from news reports, the International Shark Attack File and the Global Shark Attack File to determine which areas were more susceptible. Globally, it discovered that there have been 447 fatal shark attacks and 2,320 nonfatal incidents since 1845.

The number of reported shark attacks increased worldwide in 2010, with 79 attacks, up 25 per cent from 61 the prior year. However, consider this: in the U.S., the last decade has seen 230 deaths from dog bites and only eight from sharks.

The magazine lists the worst beaches for shark attacks as: New Smyrna Beach, Florida (238), New South Wales, Australia (55 fatalities, 171 unprovoked attacks), Second Beach, Port St. Johns, South Africa (23), Fletcher Cove, Solana Beach, CA (142), Makena, Maui (37 attacks, three fatalities), Pernambuco, Brazil (18 deaths), Sharm El Sheik, Egypt (five attacks, one fatality), Surf Beach, Vandenberg, CA; Garden Island, Western Australia; and Ponce de Leon Inlet, Florida.

One of the earliest documented shark attacks has been captured in a 1778 oil painting at the National Gallery of Art, Washington, D.C., by John Singleton Copley. *Watson and the Shark* depicts an incident that took place in Havana, Cuba, in 1749.

Brook Watson, (14), was an orphan serving as a crew member on a trading ship. On its first lunge, the shark bit a chunk of flesh off Watson's right leg below the calf; on its second attack, it removed his foot at the ankle. Watson was rescued and his leg was amputated below the knee. He went on to live a full life, including a term as Lord Mayor of London.

A deadly summer heat wave and polio epidemic occurred in the northeastern United States July 1 – 12, in 1916. Thousands of people flocked to the seaside resorts along the Jersey Shore, New Jersey to escape. The series of events that followed left four fatalities and one survivor and unfortunately changed the perception of sharks by society for decades afterwards.

Even when out of their element, sharks instill wonder and fear.

Charles Epting Vansant, (25), bled to death on the manager's desk at the Engleside Hotel in Beach Haven after he was rescued by a lifeguard from the first shark attack. His left thigh was stripped of flesh. Reports by sea captains of many sightings of large sharks off the coast of New Jersey were dismissed in the days following.

The second fatality occurred five days later 45 miles north at Beach Haven. A Swiss bellhop at the Essex & Sussex Hotel was attacked by a shark that bit him in the abdomen and severed his legs. The mutilation was so horrific that a woman on the beach notified a lifeguard that a canoe with a red hull had capsized and was floating near the surface.

Two more attacks took place on July 12 in Matawan Creek near Wyckoff dock. Lester Stillwell, (11), was grabbed while playing in the water. His friends ran to town for help and several businessmen rushed to the site and dived in searching for Stillwell's body. One of them, Watson Stanley Fisher, 24, was attacked by a shark in front of the others. His right thigh was severely injured and he bled to death on the way to the hospital.

The last victim was Joseph Dunn, (14). He was attacked a half-mile from Wyckoff dock, 30 minutes after Stillwell and Fisher. The shark grabbed his left leg but Dunn's brother and friend were able to rescue him after a vicious tug-of-war battle with the shark. He recovered from the attack.

The Jersey Shore attacks resulted in a media frenzy. Swimming declined by 75 per cent in some areas. Hundreds of sharks were landed along the East Coast after the attacks during a vendetta that was described as "the largest scale animal hunt in history," by Richard Fernicola in his book *Twelve Days of Terror.*

On July 14, Michael Schleisser, a Harlem taxidermist and Barnum and Bailey lion tamer caught a 7.5-foot (2.3 m), 325-pound (147 kg) great white shark while fishing in Raritan Bay, a few miles from Matawan Creek. Schleisser claims that the shark nearly sank his boat before he was able to kill it with a broken oar.

103

A volunteer helps to move sharks
into position for dissection.

He disemboweled his catch and discovered "suspicious fleshy material and bones" that took up "about two-thirds of a milk crate" and "together weighed fifteen pounds." Scientists identified the ingested remains as human and the shark was declared to be the Jersey maneater. No further attacks were reported along the Jersey Shore that summer. The increased presence of humans in the water was a factor in the attacks.

The Jersey Shore attacks are thought to have inspired Peter Benchley's book, *Jaws*, in 1974. In 1975 it was adapted as the film directed by Stephen Spielberg. *Jaws* was shot mostly on location in Martha's Vineyard in Massachusetts and became the highest-grossing film in history until Star Wars debuted two years later. The film made Stephen Spielberg a household name, as well as one of America's youngest multi-millionaires at the age of 26.

In the late stages of World War II in the Pacific theatre, on July 30, 1945, the USS Indianapolis, a cruiser in the U.S. navy fleet, had just delivered parts for an atomic bomb. She was torpedoed by an Imperial Japanese Navy submarine and sank in 12 minutes, leaving 900 of the 1,196 crewmembers fighting for their lives aboard the few lifeboats available or floating in the water. The navy command had no knowledge of the sinking and rescue did not arrive until three and a half days later. Only 317 survived dehydration, starvation, exposure, hypothermia, dementia and shark attacks.

Survivor Edgar Harrell shared his memories with the Bristol Herald Courier in 2008. "We'd see those shark fins swimming around us. They were as curious about us as we were them. A man would get a high fever from an injury. He would begin to hallucinate and imagine he saw an oasis. He would leave to swim to it and all of a sudden you would hear a blood-curdling scream and he would disappear. Then, his kapok [life] jacket would appear in a red pool of blood growing in the water," he said.

From business suits to ball caps, sharks
draw attention from all demographics.

In what must have been a terrifying scene for witnesses in 1952, Barry Wilson, (17), jerked suddenly before being pulled from side to side while swimming off the shore of Pacific Grove, CA. The shark lifted him completely out of the water before dragging him under.

In 1953 Rodney Fox, an Australian spearfishing champion, was defending his title when he was gripped around his waist by a great white. He struggled valiantly and was finally released. It took four hours of surgery and 360 stitches to close the wounds.

A shark attack in 1962 didn't stop underwater photographer and dive instructor LeRoy French from continuing his career. As French was floating on the surface, a 16-foot great white clamped down on his mid-section. The metal air tank dissuaded it from that attempt but it returned to bite his forearm, then his calf. It dragged him underwater and during the struggle French hit the shark in the nose with his camera equipment. His inflatable life vest popped him back up to the surface where a fellow guide hauled him back on the boat.

In the years following, French swam with hammerheads, whale sharks and many other species, but never the great white. Finally he deliberately faced his nemesis near Guadalupe Island. The dive was completed without incident, outside of a minor bump, as one of the 12-foot-long great whites swam past. French emerged with new respect and appreciation for these sharks and more understanding of their feeding habits.

Marcia Hathaway, (32), was a well-known actress in Sydney, Australia. On Jan. 29, 1963, she and six friends went on a picnic cruise to Sugarloaf Bay, in Middle Harbour. Hathaway was standing 20 feet from shore in water that was 30 inches deep when a shark attacked, almost tearing off her right leg.

107

Members of the Yarmouth County Ground
Search and Rescue Team assist with the
Yarmouth Shark Scramble annually.

Her fiancée, Frederick John Knight, (38), used his fists to fight off the shark. Her friends used sheets from the yacht as tourniquets in an attempt to stop the blood flow, then departed for Mowbray Point.

The ambulance that arrived to take her to the hospital burned out a clutch because of the steep grade and, despite 30 people desperately trying to push the vehicle, they were unable to reach the crest. A second ambulance was called. Doctors at Mater Misericordiae Hospital were unable to revive her and her friends were treated for shock. Knight later received the Stanhope Gold Medal of the British Royal Humane Society for his efforts to save Hathaway.

The day the group had set out on their picnic cruise the front page of *The Sydney Morning Herald* carried a cautionary tale under the headline: "Australia Day Holiday Surfers Warned of Sharks." The Herald reported that on the day before, beach patrol aircraft had sighted 66 sharks off the northern beaches, shark alarms were sounded at eight beaches and Narrabeen was closed for two-and-a-half hours.

In one of the first attacks captured on film, Henri Bource was swimming with two other divers off Australia in 1964 when a great white bit off his leg. His friends dragged him to safety and applied first aid. Bource says the shark released him after he gouged at its eyes and rammed his arm down its throat.

In 2010, all that was left behind from Lloyd Skinner was a pool of blood and his swimming goggles after a shark "as big as a dinosaur" and "longer than a minibus" snatched him as he swam in neck-deep water several yards from shore in Cape Town, South Africa.

A CBC cameraman films the removal of a shark's jaw
for a Land & Sea segment.

The dumping of a dead sheep from a ship is suspected of causing numerous attacks in 2010 at Sharm el Sheikh, a resort in the Red Sea. Two sharks were caught but the following day a 70-year-old German woman was killed while snorkeling.

Using common sense while in shark-frequented waters can help reduce the slight chance of attack. George H. Burgess, curator of the International Shark File, provides advice on the organization's website.
These tips include staying in groups because sharks are more likely to attack a solitary individual, avoiding swimming in murky water, refraining from splashing, not wearing wear shiny jewelry and not being in the water during twilight or night when sharks are most active.

The ISAF recommends that if you should ever find yourself under attack by a shark, there are several proactive responses. Hitting a shark on the nose, ideally with an inanimate object, usually interrupts the attack. Try to get out of the water during that time. If this is not possible, repeat bangs to the snout may again halt the attack temporarily, but will likely become increasingly less effective. If a shark actually bites, try clawing at its eyes and gills, two sensitive areas. Don't act passively if under attack - sharks respect size and power.

Announcer Cliff Gavel has a little fun with the crowd
during the Yarmouth Shark Scramble.

Chapter 10 – Shark bits & bites

Following are some interesting tidbits discovered while researching this book.

A female zebra shark at Burj Al Arab aquarium in Dubai continues to spawn baby sharks without ever mating. Although parthenogenesis or "virgin births" are known among invertebrates and some vertebrates such as hammerhead, black tip and bamboo sharks, it was unheard of for a zebra shark to display this ability. The shark, Zebedee, has been giving birth for the past four years, a first-ever for her species, says Warren Baverstock, aquarium manager at Burj Al Arab and co-author of an article featured in the *Journal of Fish Biology*.

Greenland sharks cruise at less than one mile per hour. Scientists believe that this species catches seals while they are asleep underwater. The sharks' speed might be limited by the energy costs of swimming in near-freezing water.
BBC Nature

Using shark embryos, University of Western Australia's Ocean Institute scientists have discovered that various species respond differently to different electrical impulses. Researchers say studies on shark embryos could be the key to developing an electrical repellent to keep great whites away from the shore.
ABC News

Banded bamboo sharks (chiloscyllium punctatum) are able to sense predators while still in the embryonic state. Marine neuro-ecologist Ryan Kempster, a University of Western Australia Oceans Institute PhD student, says the sharks use electrical sensors to detect predators and are able to cease respiration to avoid detection.
Science Network, Western Australia

Guests aboard a megayacht observe the shark fishing
tournament on the Yarmouth waterfront.

Great whites are the largest predatory fish on Earth. They grow to an average of 15 feet (4.6 metres) in length.
National Geographic

Of the 100-plus annual shark attacks worldwide, fully one-third to one-half are attributable to great whites. However, most of these are not fatal.
National Geographic

The great white shark may not be a common catch in Atlantic Canada, but it's not unheard of. In 1989, fishermen caught one that weighed 900 pounds. In August 2011, a 10-foot juvenile great white female was caught near Economy. A *2006 Committee On the Status of Endangered Wildlife In Canada* assessment summary cites several instances of them being discovered in either weirs or gill nets off New Brunswick, Prince Edward Island and Nova Scotia from 1950 -1990s.

Highly adapted predators, sharks have mouths lined with up to 300 serrated, triangular teeth arranged in several rows. They have an exceptional sense of smell to detect prey. They even have organs that can sense the tiny electromagnetic fields generated by animals.
National Geographic.

Multiple rows of replacement teeth grow in a groove on the inside of the jaw and steadily move forward as in a "conveyor belt;" some sharks lose 30,000 or more teeth in their lifetime. The rate of tooth replacement varies from once every eight to 10 days to several months.
Marine Education Society of Australasia

The jaws of a large great white shark can have five layers of teeth.
ReefQuest Centre for Shark Research

Some sharks, if inverted or stroked on the nose, enter a state of tonic immobility. Researchers have used this condition to handle sharks.
New World Encyclopedia

Whale sharks and spiny dogfish can live over 100 years.
Saudi Gazette

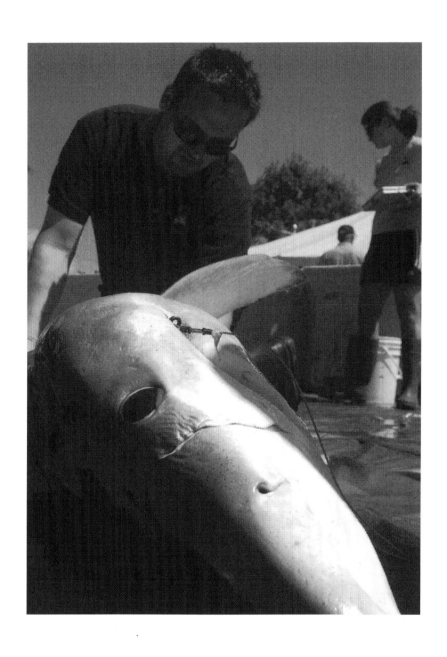

The flat stare of a dead shark doesn't deter Chris Brown.

Sharks are notoriously difficult to keep in captivity, although the Okinawa Churaumi Aquarium in Japan has been successful. From 1980 to 1998, 16 whale sharks were kept there.

The sharks were all captured around Okinawa Island by set-nets during the months of March to September and ranged in size from 3.1 to 6.3 metres, weighing between 290 and 1750 kg.
Marine Conservation News

The smallest known shark is recognized by many as the dwarf lanternshark. Smaller than the human hand, it is a little-known species of dogfish shark inhabiting the upper continental slopes off Colombia and Venezuela at depths of 950 feet.
Smithsonian National Museum of Natural History

The earliest sharks date from more than 420 million years ago, before the time of the dinosaurs.
Marine Conservation Society

The bull shark and the river shark can survive in both freshwater and seawater.
The Shark Almanac

Shortfin mako longevity is estimated at 30 years. Females take almost twice as long (19-21 years) to become sexually mature as males (7-9).
Canadian Shark Research Laboratory

Female makos give birth to live young that measure around 70 cm. They typically have between 10-15 in late winter and early spring, once every three years. Younger fish feed upon squid and bony fishes like mackerel, tuna, bonito and swordfish. Larger sharks may also eat sharks, porpoises, other marine mammals and sea turtles.
Fisheries and Oceans Canada

A scientist slices a shark's stomach open
to examine the contents.

The Scotia-Fundy Observer Program (SFOP) has maintained 100 per cent coverage of foreign fisheries in the Canadian zone since 1987. Since 1999, there have been no international long-line fisheries in Canadian waters and virtually all observed catch has been by Canadian vessels.

Most Canadian shark bycatch is taken by Scotia-Fundy vessels in swordfish and fixed gear groundfish fisheries.
Fisheries and Oceans Canada

Although shortfin mako, thresher and porbeagle have all been caught at derbies, blue sharks account for 99 per cent of all landings.
Fisheries and Oceans Canada

A total of 1,400-1,800 recreational shark fishing licences were issued between 2001 and 2002. DFO regulations state that the recreational shark fishery is to be catch-and-release only, with the exception of shark derbies.
Fisheries and Oceans Canada

Porbeagle and spiny dogfish are the only commercially fished sharks in Atlantic Canada. In 2011, 30 metric tons of the former and 125 metric tons of the latter were landed.
Fisheries and Oceans Canada

Porbeagles are among the few sharks that exhibit apparent play behaviour. Seafarers off the Cornish coast have described them rolling and repeatedly wrapping themselves in long kelp fronds near the surface, although it may be that the shark is attempting to feed on small kelp organisms or scrape off parasites. In addition, porbeagles have been seen chasing each other, and they will reportedly play with anything floating on the water.
ReefQuest Centre for Shark Research

During dissections, jaws are obtained from sharks for several
Reasons, including the determination of species and size.

The origin of the species name porbeagle is obscure. One theory is that it combines porpoise and beagle, in reference to this shark's shape and tenacious hunting habits. Other common names include Atlantic mackerel shark, beaumaris shark, and bottle-nosed shark.
English Language and Usage

The Shark Alliance is a coalition of more than 100 conservation, scientific and recreational organizations dedicated to restoring and conserving shark populations by improving shark conservation policies.

Every October, members of the Shark Alliance in Europe conduct a week of public activities to promote shark appreciation and to call for conservation measures. For details of the annual European Shark Week, visit www.europeansharkweek.org

Cage diving with sharks was banned in Western Australia following the deaths of four people attacked while in the sea between September 2011 and July 2012. The activity is popular in Southern Australia and South Africa but operators are now prevented from setting up businesses on Australia's west coast for fear of attracting more sharks.
The Daily Telegraph

In Southwest Nova Scotia, fishing is often a family affair.

Chapter 11 Finis for finning

Sharks are slaughtered for their teeth, jaws, skin to make leather shoes and belts, liver for oil, and cartilage for purported cancer cures. Derivatives from sharks are also used in cosmetics, skin care products and in medicines. But the most senseless of all shark deaths is their killing for the sole purpose of their fins.

Legend has it that shark fin soup was created by an emperor in the Sung Dynasty (AD 968) who wanted to impress upon others his wealth, power and generosity.

The expensive delicacy is served in China and other countries. Shark fin – similar to a brand name car or bag – became known as a conspicuous consumption product. It is reputed to bring good fortune to those who dine on it and to reflect the wealth and importance of the host who serves it - a public display of social status.

The thick soup consists of chicken and ham broth, shredded chicken and shark fin (which is tasteless). Once processed, fibres from the fins give the soup a glutinous consistency. The price, depending on whether the fin is whole or in pieces, can range from $5 to $2,000 a bowl. The type of shark has a bearing on the price as well.

Many consumers are unaware of the issue because shark fin is called Yu Chi in Chinese, which literally translates into English as fish wing.

An estimated 70 million sharks are caught annually to fill the bowls of those of those who consume this dish. The sharks are hauled aboard the boats, their fins are sliced off, then the body is thrown back into the ocean while still alive. Fishing vessels do this at sea to increase profitability and fill their holds with lucrative fins as opposed to bodies that have little value.

The practice of finning occurs worldwide and is most common in high-seas fisheries.

A volunteer oversees the weighing.

Fishing fleets target valuable fish such as tuna, using thousands of baited hooks on miles of long-line, and freeze their catch onboard. Unfortunately, long-liners often catch several times as many sharks than they do tuna.

Shark bycatch has long been considered a nuisance and sharks were cut loose and allowed to swim away.

However, as shark fins have become increasingly valuable, fewer sharks are being released. Bycatch is often not officially landed at ports, therefore data on the extent of the trade are limited. Traditionally Hong Kong was the centre for shark fin imports, although the economic rise of China has seen an increase in imports through mainland routes making accurate tracking of trade in shark fins more difficult.

In small inshore fisheries in tropical countries, sun-drying of fins requires minimal technology and artisanal fishermen are encouraged by shark fin traders to target local populations of sharks. As a result, even coastal shark populations in the remotest parts of the world are now vulnerable to over-exploitation, and rapid depletion of local shark populations often results from such trading activity.

The fins are now among the most expensive seafood products in the world, fetching up to $676 per kilogram. Shark species that are commonly finned are sandbar, bull, hammerhead, blacktip, porbeagle, mako, thresher, whale, blue sharks and occasionally white sharks.

One pectoral fin from a whale shark can sell for up to $100,000 US and a basking shark pectoral fin fetched $250,000.

Thought to be an aphrodisiac in some parts of the world, shark fin soup can actually cause infertility. The fins may contain toxic methyl-mercury. The limit for consumption of methyl-mercury, set by the Environmental Protection Agency, is 0.1 microgram per kilogram of body weight. Studies have shown shark meat contains as much as 1,400 micrograms of methyl-mercury in one kg. A person weighing 155 lbs. could therefore get 50 times the legal amount in one single portion of shark steak.

125

Media coverage of shark related events is always popular.

A large number of countries now prohibit finning, although international waters are unregulated. The conservation drive continues with protective legislation on a rising trend.

Taiwan banned shark finning in 2011. The Peninsula Hotel, a legendary Hong Kong landmark, banned shark fin soup effective January 1, 2012.

The Wall Street Journal also reported at that time that the luxury Shangri-La hotel chain is banning shark fin from all of its 72 hotels, most of which are in Asia.

The Marine conservation group WildAid says about 95 per cent of all shark fin is consumed within China. Supermarket chains FairPrice and Carrefour have halted the sale of shark fin, as well as ColdStorage, another chain with several outlets in Singapore.

In June, 2012, Venezuela banned shark finning in its waters and established a 1,440-square-mile shark sanctuary in the Caribbean Sea surrounding the Los Roques Archipelago.

Hong Kong Disneyland dropped shark fin soup from its wedding banquet menu after international pressure from environmental groups, who threatened to boycott its parks worldwide. The University of Hong Kong has banned shark fin soup on campus.

On Jan.1, 2012, legislation took effect in Oregon and California, banning the sale, possession and distribution of shark fins and related products.

In June, 2012 , a high school science teacher and his former student set out from Paso Robles, CA, to cycle across five states in support of sharks. Funds raised through the Spinning to End Finning initiative were to be donated to Pretoma, an award-winning organization supported by the Monterey Bay Aquarium.

Canines in the crowd are just as interested as their owners
at shark fishing tournaments.

Sea Shepherd Singapore has been educating the public for the last several years about the devastating effect that the Asian culture's use of shark fin soup is having on shark populations. A series of striking postcards has been produced and is being marketed widely with the objective of stopping the cruel tradition.

Founded in 2009, Shark Truth is a grassroots nonprofit organization dedicated to promoting awareness, education and action for sharks. Its philosophy is to create long-term champions from within the community to protect sharks and oceans. The organization created a unique campaign: the Happy Hearts Love Sharks wedding contest, which encourages betrothed couples to break tradition and make their wedding banquet fin free. Participants have their names entered in a draw for a grand prize trip south to an ecotourism destination. Shark Truth estimates it has saved at least 2,800 sharks from being eaten by diverting 28,000 bowls of shark fin from consumption.

The Canadian Fisheries Act prohibits fishermen from finning, but most of Canada allows the import of shark fins (except from endangered species).

Shark Stewards, a non-profit shark conservation organization based in the San Francisco Bay Area, provide a legislative toolkit to facilitate effective advocacy for shark conservation. The downloadable "FIN-Free" Toolkit, designed to educate and empower citizens, restaurant owners and legislators to unite against shark finning, is available on SharkStewards.org.

About the author

Carla Allen is an award-winning reporter for The Vanguard, a community newspaper in Yarmouth, Nova Scotia.

Some of her happiest moments have been at sea, including working for a week banding lobsters on her cousin's boat, the Scalded Witch; sailing across the Gulf of Maine aboard an 80-foot ketch in the Yarmouth Cup race; travelling from Yarmouth to Bar Harbor with Spike Hampson as part of his riverboat odyssey; or simply paddling about the local harbour in her kayak.

21092742R00072